Boat Ropes

Boat Ropes

A Guide
to the
Use of Rope and Lines
on
Sailing Cruisers

Bill Finnis

WATERLINE

Published by Waterline Books
an imprint of Airlife Publishing Ltd.
101 Longden Road, Shrewsbury, England

ISBN 1 85310 509 0

A Sheerstrake production.

A CIP catalogue record of this book
is available from the British Library.

Photographs by Les Nunn (except P.92).
Illustrations by Bill Finnis.

Printed by Livesey Ltd., Shrewsbury, England.

Also by Bill Finnis
The Passage Maker's Manual

Contents

Chapter 1

Knots and Ropework

It is satisfying to have scores of knots at your fingertips but not all will be essential to the well-being of your boat. Make a start with six or eight suitable knots and get them so embedded in your subconscious that you no longer have to pause for thought when you wish to construct them. There is only one way to reach this stage and that is to practise daily until you no longer have to think about what your fingers are doing.

It is important to use a suitable piece of line for your knot-making practise sessions. Line that has a diameter of ten or maybe twelve millimetres is big enough to show what has been done and yet is light enough to be manipulated easily. A metre will be sufficient for most purposes and it will help if both ends are heat sealed.

Once you have a basic repertoire of knots literally at your finger tips, the chances are that you will want to learn more and that is no bad thing for a yachtsman.

Before we launch ourselves into the construction of various knots, bends and hitches there are a few terms, which if understood, will make the task much easier.

Standing Part
This part of the rope is the end that does not move, usually because it is secured or fixed to a point.

Running Part
This is the other end of the rope if it is normally free to move.

A halyard used to hoist a sail will illustrate the point. One end of the halyard will be attached to the head of the sail and this is called the standing part, as in relation to the sail it does not move. The other end is the running part – except that nautical custom decrees that in this case we call it a fall!

Working Part
In what follows, the working part will indicate the end of the line that is manipulated in the construction of the knot.

(South Paws, I'm sorry but I must ask you to read left for right and right for left, but then I guess you have figured out for yourself what an unjust world this is!)

Bitter End
This is the extreme end of a length of line. It is also used more specifically to name the last piece of line to come off a coil of new rope.

Incidentally if you are taking new line from a new coil of rope, or even a ball of string for that matter, take it from the centre of the coil. In that way the coil will retain its shape almost to the very end.

Bight

When a rope is bent to form an open 'U' shape it is called a bight. In itself a bight has no purpose but it often forms part of the construction of a knot. In earlier days a bight was called a bend from which certain knots derive their title of 'bend', for example, the sheet bend. A bight that is closed becomes either a round turn or a half hitch

Round Turn

Exactly as its name suggests, this is a rope turned 360° around a spar, a bollard, a ring or another rope.

Half Hitch

This is really a round turn but whereas the round turn is made around a spar or post, the half hitch is not necessarily made around anything. The half hitch is seldom of use by itself but is often an important part of other knots.

Overhand or Thumb Knot

This is the first step in the construction of a reef knot and is an important part of the fisherman's knot. By itself it can be used as a stopper knot, i.e. it will stop a line pulling through a hole. When used in this way in very thin line the overhand knot often does not make enough bulk to be effective and it is better to resort to a figure of eight knot.

Fig 1 *The Overhand or Thumb Knot*

Figure of Eight Knot

Really an overhand knot with an extra turn to it that creates the necessary volume to allow it to function as a stopper knot.

Fig 2 *The Figure of Eight Knot*

Fisherman's Knot

I find the fisherman's knot especially useful. It will unite two lines of approximately the same diameter most efficiently and yet can still be undone easily, the hallmark of a good knot. Its construction is simplicity itself, an overhand knot in the end of both pieces of line each with the other length of line trapped within the overhand knot. A point to watch is that the short ends of the lines emerge from the overhand knots as shown in the illustration, so that they allow the knots to 'sit comfortably back to back'.

If the line used to make the fisherman's knot is particularly slippery, a figure of eight knot can be used in place of the overhand knot. Additional turns mean extra friction and in work friction is often what is needed to help the knot do its job.

Fig 3 *The Fisherman's Knot*

Clove Hitch

Two half hitches arranged as in the illustration will form a clove hitch which can be made around a spar or another rope, around a ring or be dropped over a bollard, although there are better knots that can be used for this latter purpose.

Under load a clove hitch will slide along a spar or rope if the pull is in the same direction as the spar to which it is attached, it can only resist a pull away from the spar at a large angle. For a line to maintain its position on a spar or rope when the pull is roughly in line with it a different knot must be used.

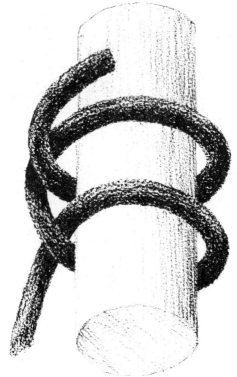

Fig 4 *The Clove Hitch*

Spar Hitch

The spar hitch is similar to the clove hitch but it is a constrictor knot and as such is more secure under load and on a slippery spar. Despite the grip this knot affords it is easy to release. Like the clove hitch the spar hitch will slide if subjected to a pull in the direction of the spar.

Fig 5 *The Spar Hitch*

Rolling Hitch

This knot will resist a sideways pull in one direction. It is really a clove hitch with an extra round turn to the first half hitch. This double turn must be positioned so that the running part of the line engages with it when the load comes onto the rope and it must cross the first half hitch to lock the knot on that side. Just occasionally I have found that a third round turn has been needed for the rolling hitch to maintain its position under load on a particularly slippery spar or rope. Unlike the clove hitch the rolling hitch will remain in position when the load is parallel with the spar or rope on which it is made but it can only resist sliding in one direction.

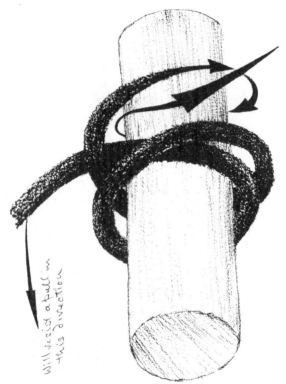

Will resist a pull in this direction

Fig 6 The Rolling Hitch

Camel Hitch

The little known camel hitch will resist movement in either direction but can easily be slid along the spar or rope on which it is made up if its position needs to be changed.

It seems that camels are moored by having their head rope fastened to a line which is pegged to the ground. It is the camel hitch that is used for this purpose because it allows the keeper to adjust the camel's position on the ground line but it will not move either way along the line when it is under load.

The camel hitch is started by making three round turns side by side with the working end on another rope or spar. The working end is then taken to the far side of the running part where a clove hitch is made to complete the knot.

Fig 7 *The Camel Hitch*

Sheet Bend

This is used to join two lines together. They need not be the same size but if the diameters differ then the larger must be used to form the bight that is the start of the sheet bend.

Fig 8A *The Sheet Bend*

If there is a danger of the sheet bend slipping under load – some modern fibres are prone to this – then a second turn can be taken to form a 'double sheet bend'. The double version should also be used if there is a marked difference between the diameters of the two lines to be joined.

Fig 8B *The Double Sheet Bend*

21

Reef Knot

This is not a totally reliable knot, so much so that it is a friend of the conjuring fraternity. However it does have its use and as its name suggests it is needed when reefing a sail. The reefing points that are tied under the foot of the sail to retain and tidy up the reefed part are secured with a reef knot. Whilst performing this duty the reef knot is under no great strain nor is it jiggled about and the fact that it comes apart easily when it is no longer needed is a welcome asset.

This knot is made by joining the ends of two pieces of line or both ends of one piece of line and the usual instruction given is 'left over right' which will make an overhand knot, followed by 'right over left' to complete it. The illustration shows what the finished knot should look like. It is important to note how each pair of lines emerge from their bights side by side. If one part comes up through the bight and its partner goes down through the same bight you have made the much despised 'granny knot'! The granny does not lie as flat as the reef, looks untidy and is even more unreliable and perversely it can be difficult to release, apart from that there is not much wrong with it !

Sometimes when the first part of the reef knot is made it refuses to stay as tight as you would wish whilst you complete the knot, the moment the tension is relaxed the first step starts to slip. If the initial step is given two turn instead of one it will usually stay put when the tension is off. If you add a second turn to the final step to keep things tidy the reef knot becomes a 'surgeon's knot'.

Fig 9 *The Reef Knot*

Bowline

The bowline is a most useful non-slip loop, it is in effect, a sheet bend made in the end of one piece of line.

There are a number of ways to make a bowline but there is only one seamanlike method and it pays to work at it until you can tie it with your eyes shut. It may help if I break down the moves into single steps.

23

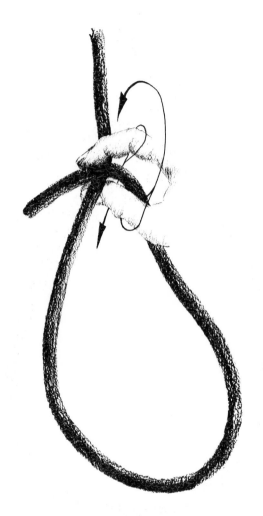

Fig 10A

Step 1

Make a bight with one end of your line which we shall call the working part. The bight should be no longer than the loop you need. When you make this bight, cross the working part of the line over the running part to your left.(Fig 10A)

24

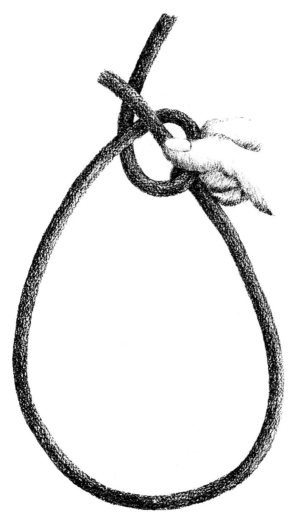

Fig 10B

Step 2
With the thumb of the hand inside the bight, grip the lines at
the cross-over point with the index finger on top and the
thumb beneath.(Fig 10B)

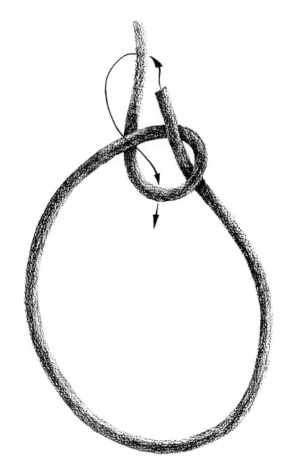

Fig 10C

Step 3
Whilst grasping the lines in this way, rotate the right hand away from you so that the palm is now uppermost. If all has gone well you will have created a small circle in the line and the working part should now be pointing upwards through the centre of the circle. Don't move on until you can carry out these first three steps faultlessly.(Fig 10C)

Fig 10D

Step 4

With the working part laying parallel to the running part
change your grip on it so that you can pass that end behind
the running part to your left and then back down through
the same circle that it came from. Snug everything down and
you should have a bowline.(Fig 10D)

27

During World War Two the Navy required us to be able to make a bowline around our body with one hand just in case we found ourselves taking an involuntary swim. This was to be done whilst the other hand was hanging on to the rope that had, hopefully, been thrown to us from the deck of a passing vessel. When you have mastered the bowline I would urge you to learn to do this , it just may save your life one day. Even if you have no cause to test its life-saving qualities you will have a party trick with which to amaze your friends.

Single-Handed Bowline

This is made with the right hand whilst the left hand reaches up and grasps the rope as high as is comfortably possible. This will leave the rope below the left hand slack so that it can be manipulated. If you have mastered the method for the construction of a bowline as described previously, the two accompanying illustrations should clarify the steps.

Step 1

Pass the line around your body from left to right and hold onto the running part with your left hand.

Step 2

Holding the working part in your right hand, coax the slack line below your left hand into a small bight around your right wrist. Pass the end around the running part and pull it down through the small bight.(Figs 11A & B)

Two things could cause problems. Don't reach up the line and hang from it, remember, if it is for real you will be floating in the water and secondly, you could cause yourself difficulty by not allowing enough slack line in step two.

Fig 11A

Fig 11B

There are a number of different bowlines, the 'spanish bowline', 'bowline on the bight' and the 'running bowline'. They are not essential but can just occasionally make a useful contribution and if you have really mastered the bowline the others will quickly fall into place.

Running Bowline

This gives a noose that can be altered as you wish but will not lock in that position. It is made by making a very small bowline around the running part.

Fig 12 *The Running Bowline*

Some of the bowlines that are outlined below can be used as bosun's chairs. Man-made fibre ropes are excellent but they can be rather slippery. If one of these bowlines is to be used to raise a man up a mast I think it would be prudent to add two half hitches to lock the bowline with total certainty. When the knot is forming ensure that the working part will be long enough to allow you to add two half hitches around the adjacent part of the bight.

Double Bowline
This is a form of bowline that will, as its name suggests, give a double bight instead of the more usual single. The size of either bight can be increased but only at the expense of reducing the other bight. Its main use is as an emergency bosun's chair.

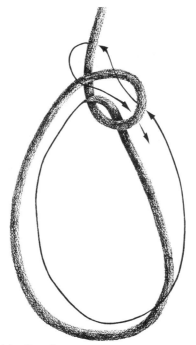

Fig 13 *The Double Bowline*

The double bowline starts with the first three steps of the normal bowline except that the length of the working part needs to be long enough to form two big bights.

When the first three steps are completed the working part is pulled part way through the small circle from above until there is enough line to allow you to pass the end of the working part up through the small circle for the second time. The bowline is then completed in the normal way.

Bowline on the Bight

Double the last six feet of a length of line, treat it as if it was a single piece of line and carry out steps one, two and three in the original bowline instructions, using the doubled part of the line as the working part.

You should now have the bitter end of the doubled line poking through the circle.

Pull the doubled line through sufficiently to allow you to reach through the bight thus formed and grip the major, double strand bight.

Pull the large double strand bight and then cause the single strand bight to settle above the small circle which started the knot. Snug everything down and the result should be a bowline with two bights of fixed length which can be adjusted if the knot is slackened off a little.

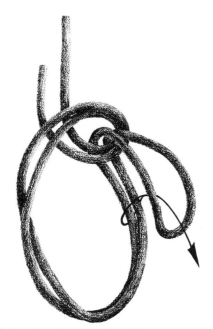

Fig 14A *Step 1 The Bowline on the Bight*

Fig 14B *Step 2 The Bowline on the Bight*

Spanish Bowline

This is not what is generally accepted to be a bowline, its construction is quite different. I have included it here because it is called a bowline and when completed the knot presents two adjustable bights that can be used in much the same way as the double bowline.

Three half hitches are laid out as in Figure15A. The major loop is capsized towards you so as to encompass the smaller loops, then each side is taken under the nearest small loop and drawn up through it,Figure15B. When all is snugged down the knot should look as in Figure15C.

Fig 15A *Step 1 The Spanish Bowline*

Fig 15B *Step 2 The Spanish Bowline*

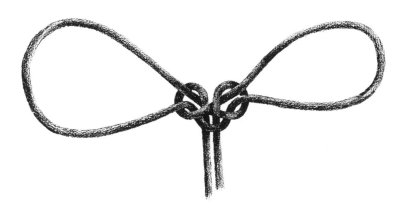

Fig 15C *Step 3 The Spanish Bowline*

35

Bargee Hitch

A sound, useful knot that deserves to be more widely used. It can be made equally well in rope or chain. This hitch is made around a bollard or samson post when securing a mooring line inboard. One often sees a clove hitch used in this situation but it is not really suited to the job. The least load on a line that is made fast with a clove hitch will make it extremely difficult to release and once it is released you no longer have control over the load which may prove to be too much for you to handle.

The bargee hitch can be freed no matter what the load imposed on it and what is more, because the hitch is started with three round turns the load can be held with ease even though the locking bight has been removed, the friction of those three round turns will allow you to hold an enormous load. If the line needs to be eased (surged) you can, by removing one or perhaps two turns, allow the line to pay out without losing control. Once you are ready to cast off, all that is needed is to throw off the remaining turns.

The hitch is made by placing three round turns on the samson post. Next a bight of line or chain is passed under the line that is leading away from the post and brought up and dropped over the samson post. Make sure that the half hitch is arranged as in the illustration, that way it will lock itself in place.

The same hitch can be used to secure a halyard or sheet to its winch barrel with far less fuss than is involved in using many cleats. We have sailed for days on end with our sheets secured in this fashion and they have required no attention at all.

Fig 16 *The Bargee Hitch*

Round Turn and Two Half Hitches

This knot starts with a turn around a spar, bollard or mooring ring and then the working end is used to make a clove hitch (the two half hitches) around the running part of the line. When releasing the knot the round turn can give a measure of control but of course the single round turn will not give anything like the same amount of control as the three round turns of the bargee hitch.

Fig 17 *The Round Turn and Two Half Hitches*

Fisherman's Bend or Anchor Bend

Not unlike the round turn and two half hitches except that
the first half hitch is taken under the round turn. This is a
very secure knot, the heavier the load the greater the
restraining load imposed on the first half hitch by the round
turn. It is used primarily to bend a line to a kedge anchor.
One often sees a bowline used for this purpose but a bowline
can move freely on the ring of the anchor and could, given
time, chafe through. The anchor bend cannot do this as it is
held securely to the anchor ring.

Fig 18 The Fisherman's Bend or Anchor Bend

Heaving-Line

I stand in wonder that something so simple as throwing a heaving-line can be done so badly so frequently.

More often than not one sees a single coil of rope thrown to the shore in a vain attempt to reach a willing pair of hands. It is doomed to failure. You can see it on any weekend and still the throwers do not question their technique.

The answer is as simple as it is spectacular. Make two coils of the line, if you are right handed hold the first coil in the right hand and the second in your left hand retaining the inboard end in the fingers of the left hand.

Throw the right hand coil and allow the left hand coil to follow the first, but do retain the end!

By this means a heaving-line of some twelve fathoms (25 metres) can be thrown to its full length every time. By the way, it is considered good nautical manners to direct the heaving-line to one side of the recipient, not straight at him!

A mooring line can be thrown in the same way, indeed it is the only method to throw any line successfully.

We keep our heaving-line on two hooks in the dog house and over the years it has proved its worth to both ourselves and others in need.

Twelve fathoms (25 metres) of six to ten millimetre diameter line will serve well for a heaving-line. Work an eye splice about 6in(15cm) into one end and a monkey's fist into the other. A four stranded monkey's fist made around a 1¼in (4cm) diameter wooden ball is about right for a six millimetre line and three strands will serve for a ten millimetre line.

Monkey's Fist

To make a three stranded monkey's fist lay down three concentric circles of line as in Figure 19A. The line to the top of the picture is the running part and the line to the left is the working part.

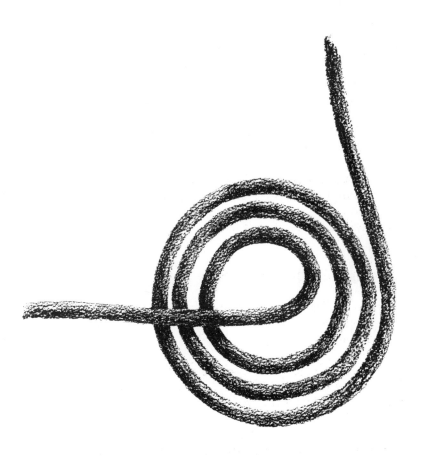

Fig 19A *Step 1 Monkey's Fist*

Wrap the working part round the concentric circles three times, finally bringing the working part underneath everything to make its appearance at the right of the coils as in Figure 19B.

Fig 19b *Step 2 Monkey's Fist*

The working part must now be taken under the parts you have just wrapped around the original circles of line and three more turns must be made around the horizontal turns as in Figure 19C.

Fig 19c *Step 3 Monkey's Fist*

All that remains now is to take all the slack out of the knot until the whole thing is tight and then either splice or seize the working part to the running part as in Figure 19D.

Fig 19D *Step 4 Monkey's Fist*

Useful Knots That Happen to be Decorative

There is a group of knots that are often called decorative knots and I think that this is a great pity. That they are decorative is beyond dispute and they are often used as adornment and embellishment. However, their prime purpose is, or almost certainly was when they were designed, to satisfy some practical need and they will still satisfy those needs.

The 'Turk's Head' for example , can be used for a stop on a dinghy oar or to indicate amidships on a steering wheel. Other uses may be on the forestay to prevent piston hanks sliding down and jamming on the bottle screw at the foot of the stay, on the top of your anchor winch handle, at the end of the tiller on your outboard motor or to take chafe on the whisker pole where it clashes with the shrouds. The list is as long as your needs and your imagination, and so it is with other so called decorative knots.

I would not advocate the indiscriminate use of these knots simply as a form of decoration; used in that way they become seagoing versions of gold chains and garden gnomes. But used where they serve a practical purpose they help to give a boat a seamanlike nautical air that is often missing from many current production yachts.

Turk's Head

There are a number of ways to make a Turk's head. They all give the same result but because there are several ways to approach the knot it is wise to stick with one set of illustrations until you have mastered the beast.

Photo A shows the Turk's head in use as an oar stop.
Photo B shows a three strand Turk's head made in stiff line so that it can be slipped off the spar around which it has been made to show the all round construction, note the pattern that you should be working towards.

45

Boat Ropes

Photo A

Photo B

To be easy on yourself make your initial attempts around a fixed spar. If you attempt to make it around a moveable spar you will be adding just another problem at a time when additional problems are not wanted.

For ease of working, the line and the spar should bear some relationship to each other and a 6 millimetre diameter line suits a spar of about 1½in(40mm) to 1¾in(45mm) diameter, a rolling pin happens to be about this size.

Two turns must be made around the spar as shown in Figure 20A which will lead on to the result in Figure 20B shown on the next page.

Fig 20A *Step 1 Turk's Head*

Fig 20B *Step 2 Turk's Head*

When this point is reached bights 'A' and 'B' must be manipulated as indicated by the arrows, taking 'A' over 'B'. The working part 'C' is now passed through the bight made by 'B' from the left and then through the bight of 'A' from the right, Figure 20c.

Fig 20C *Step 3 Turk's Head*

When this is done, rotate the knot around the spar a little so that you can see what is happening at the back. The end with which you started should be apparent and if 'C' is laid alongside this end, but on a reciprocal course, it should be possible to follow it round the Turk's head, building up the knot into however many strands you may wish.

49

Both the 'Wall' and 'Crown' knots are used to form parts of other knots. In making both these knots the three strands of the rope must be separated from each other for a suitable distance but the end of each strand must be heat sealed before you start to unlay the line.

A temporary whipping, or at least a 'whipping' of masking tape, must be secured to the rope's end at the point beyond which you do not wish the rope to unlay, before attempting to part the three strands.

When laying up these knots go in the direction of the lay of the rope.

In addition to helping to form other knots the wall knot can be used by itself as a stopper knot, as can the 'manrope knot'. In this respect they are no different from the overhand and figure of eight knots but they do have a more decorative and permanent air to them and should be used accordingly.

Wall Knot

To start the wall knot pass strand 1 behind the strand to its left - strand 2. Next take strand 2 and pass it beneath strands 1 and 3 as shown in Figure 21A.

Finally pass strand 3 below strands 2 and 1 and then bring it up through the bight initially made by strand 1 as in Figure 21B.

When all the strands are pulled up comfortably tight you will have a single wall knot.

If the wall knot is to be used as a stopper knot, it is usual to give it greater bulk by following around with each strand to produce a double wall knot.

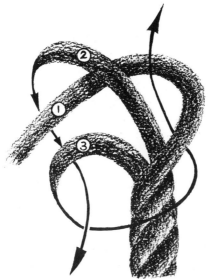

Fig 21A *Step 1 Wall Knot*

Fig 21B *Step 2 Wall Knot*

Fig 21C *Step 3 The finished Wall Knot*

Once the single wall knot has been formed, but before it is pulled up tight, strand 3 should be made to lie alongside strand 2 following its progress under both 1 and 3. Strand 2 must stay adjacent to strand 1 passing under strands 3 and 2. Finally strand 1 must follow the course of strand 3 by passing under 2 and 1.

When all has been pulled up snug, a whipping will be needed to hold the three strands together above the knot.

Crown Knot

This knot serves no useful purpose on its own as it does not lock securely but it is a necessary component of some other knots.

Make a vertical bight with strand 2 and pass the end of the strand 1 through it retaining both bights 1 and 2.

Strand 3 is passed behind 2 and into the bight made by 1.

Fig 22 *The Crown Knot*

Manrope Knot

This consists of a double wall and crown, indeed it is sometimes called a 'wall and crown knot'.

The first step is to make a slack wall knot which is surmounted by a crown knot. The strands are then allowed to follow round the original knots so doubling up each of them. The tails of the three strands must be passed down through the centre of the knot until they issue from the bottom of it.

When the knot is snugged up tight the ends can be cut off, spliced into the rope below the knot or tapered and held in place with a length of whipping.

Fig 23 *The Manrope Knot*

Chapter 2
Whipping and Seizing

Tapering synthetic lines is not easy. In this respect, and in others too, natural fibre ropes were nicer to work with. The manrope knot locks so well that it is perfectly reasonable to cut the tails off and use a hot soldering iron to seal the ends of the cut fibres.

Ropes' Ends
Rope ends must be secured against unlaying and there are a variety of ways of doing this.

Chandlers sell short lengths of thin plastic tubing that are intended to be placed onto the end of a rope and then shrunk into place by the application of a little heat, usually a lighted match. Whilst they stay in position they work but in my experience they don't stay long enough.

For centuries seamen have applied whippings of very thin line to rope ends to hold them together and they work as well today as they ever did.

Modern ropes are made of plastic fibres which melt when heated and it is usual to heat seal the ends of each length of line. Chandlers will use a purpose made gadget but we can resort to a gas lighter of the kind that produces a flame or alternatively a soldering iron can be used. For all except the smallest line a match does not produce enough heat to do the job.

Whilst heat sealing gives a reasonable result it pays to apply a whipping to back it up. The strands of the old vegetable fibre ropes retain the twist that the manufacturer imparts to them and this helps the rope to hold together while you work on it. Most man-made fibres are not so helpful and will unlay given the slightest chance. The only answer seems to be to heat seal the ends before starting to work on a synthetic fibre rope.

Some synthetic whipping twines are very slippery and this can cause difficulties when working with them. To overcome this, pull the twine across a small block of beeswax, a candle will serve but beeswax is better. When coated like this the slipperiness will disappear.

Common Whipping
Lay a bight of whipping twine along the length of the rope that is to be whipped so that the closed end of the bight is pointing towards the end of the rope and lies close to it as in Figure 24A.

Using the working part of the whipping twine, bind the rope's end tightly with it, leaving the tail of the bight exposed. When there are sufficient turns on the rope's end, pass the working part through the bight and pull up tight. Pull on the tail of the bight until the bight and a little of the working part of the twine disappears beneath the whipping and cut off the spare twine.The result should look like Figure 24B.

Fig 24A *Step 1 Common Whipping*

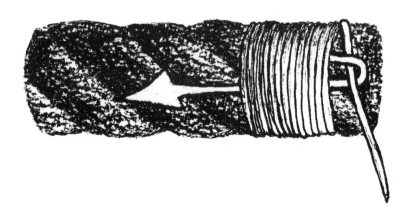

Fig 24B *Completed Common Whipping*

Palm and Needle Whipping

You will need a sailmaker's palm and needle for this whipping. The needle is triangular in section for its lower half and it, and the palm, are usually available at most yacht chandlers. The sailmaker's palm is a shaped band of stout leather that is intended to fit around the palm of your hand. Where the band of leather crosses your palm there is a shallow cup of metal to allow you to push hard on the head of the needle to make it penetrate the rope or fabric on which you are working. In other words it serves the same purpose as the needlewoman's thimble.

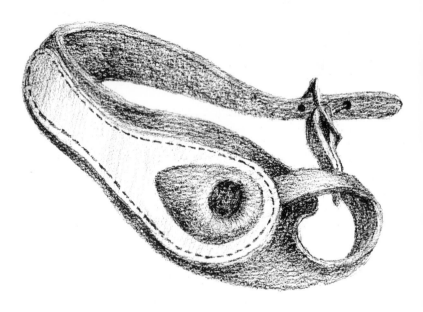

Fig 25 *The Sailmaker's Palm*

There are two patterns of palm offered for sale. One has a strap on the back to allow you to adjust it to fit your hand. The other is of fixed size and appears not to fit every hand. Naturally the adjustable version is dearer, but as it will last a lifetime it is worth paying the extra.

All the palms I have ever seen offered for sale are so stiff as to raise a blister in no time at all. The trick here is to soak the new palm in olive or vegetable cooking oil for a day or two when it will become quite soft and supple.

The palm and needle whipping is my first choice if I am whipping a rope end. With the needle threaded, pass it through part of the rope about an inch from the end of the line, more for a thick line and less for a thinner line, simply to anchor the one end. Lay on the whipping turns and then pass the needle and thread through the rope behind a strand.(Fig 26A)

Bring the whipping twine diagonally down the adjacent contline (the spiral interval between the strands of the rope) to the bottom of the whipping. From here the needle must be passed behind the next strand of rope where the twine is brought diagonally up to the top of the whipping along the contline.(Fig 26B) These steps are repeated until each contline is overlaid with a length of whipping twine. The end of the twine is then passed through the rope to secure it.

There is a whipping called 'Sailmakers Whipping' which looks like a palm and needle whipping but its construction does not require a palm or needle. Its disadvantage is that the ends of the rope cannot be heat sealed before you start work on the whipping because in the final stages a bight of the whipping twine must be dropped over each of the three strands. This was fine with the old vegetable fibre ropes but it becomes all but impossible with most of the ropes that are composed of man-made fibres because of their tendency to unlay.

Fig 26A *Step 1 Palm and Needle Whipping*

Fig 26B *Step 2 Palm and Needle Whipping*

French Whipping

This is both effective and decorative. It is started with a clove hitch and then followed by a series of half hitches until the required area is covered. Give the ends of the whipping twine a gentle touch with a small soldering iron to melt them just enough to make them adhere to the main body of the whipping.

If all has gone well, the half hitches will form a continuous spiral along and around the rope on which it has been made. If the continuity of the spiral is broken it will be because you made at least one half hitch at that point in the wrong direction. A change in the direction of the spiralling ridge can be made deliberately by this means, if the whipping is to be used decoratively.

French whipping can also be used effectively in a number of different situations. As with knots that happen to be decorative, so it is with some whippings and French whipping is one of these.

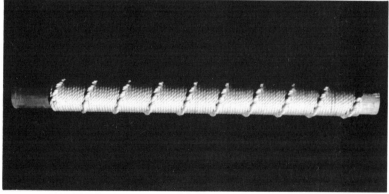

French Whipping

When an electric cable is to be run up a stanchion post, most people reach for a roll of insulating tape. Three weeks later the tape has become a set of Irish pennants flying in the breeze. Instead of tape, try lengths of French whipping. Use three millimetre diameter line and seal the ends at the start and finish in place with a hot soldering iron. Give it a coat of paint and the whipping will last as long as your boat, and look good too. If you really want to make a tiddley job of it put a Turk's head at either end.

Split plastic tubing is often slipped onto shrouds, guard rails and the like to protect sails and ropes against chafe, especially necessary in a vessel that is to be used for long distance sailing. To get the tubing in place a cut must be made along the length of the tube. Again the dreaded insulating tape is so often called into use. A few short lengths of French whipping or two or three Turk's heads will serve so much better.

The metal of a steering wheel is cold and for my taste too slim for a comfortable grip. One of the whippings will transform it both to the touch and visually too. Again three millimetre line is about right. Use a Turk's head to mark the top of the wheel when the rudder is in the fore and aft position.

Seizings

Braidline has justly become popular for sheets and halyards, but for me at least, it is a beast to splice. An eye splice is what is usually needed. Typically the instructions for the construction of an eye splice in braidline will run to five pages in a book that needs less than one page to outline the formation of an eye splice in three stranded rope. For me there are but two solutions. Either pay a professional to do the job or resort to a seizing.

Round Seizings

Form the eye you need and include a thimble if you intend to make a hard eye. Using the palm and needle sew the two parts of the line together, starting just below the eye and continuing for about forty millimetres. The sewing will need to be strong but its appearance is not important as it will be covered by the seizing.

Secure the seizing twine to the rope just below the eye. Apply sufficient turns, each one close to the last and pulling each turn very tight before laying the next. When you have sufficient turns in place secure the twine with a half hitch around both parts of the rope and then lay on a second layer of turns. This second layer must be tight, but not so tight as to cause the turns to lose themselves amongst the turns of the first layer. The second layer should be two turns less than the first to ensure that the ends do not slip off the first layer.

Finish the seizing by taking the twine through the eye and down the length of the seizing, up and back again to the eye as is shown in the racking seizing illustration (Fig 27B). Lay on two or three round turns like this, hauling taught each turn as it is applied. Secure the end of the whipping twine.

Racking Seizing

This is made in much the same way as the round seizing but with figure of eight rather than round turns and has just one layer of turns. The construction of a racking seizing precludes the possibility of sewing the rope together but the seizing is strong enough without it. We have sailed many thousands of miles with the eyes in our jib sheets secured with a pair of racking seizings and have never yet had one fail. We use a pair of seizings out of respect for "Finnis' Principle of Permanent Pessimism". If one seizing fails, there is another waiting to take over its job.

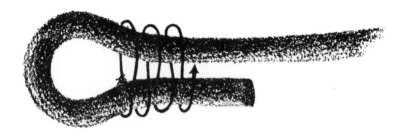

Fig 27A *Step 1 Racking Seizing*

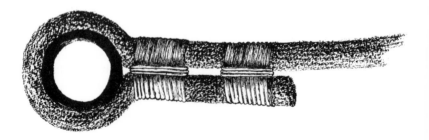

Fig 27B *Completed pair of Racking Seizings*

Both the described seizings need to be pulled up very tight and a serving mallet is the appropriate tool to use. The only snag with this advice is that a request for a serving mallet at your local chandlery will likely be greeted with a glassy stare. An alternative would be to use a marlin spike and a marlin spike hitch. Personally I have found a stout gardening glove to be more than adequate. True, it doesn't have the same nautical ring to it but why should we not borrow and adapt? After all, the hoe, the tool that was designed to remove barnacles from a boat's bottom is increasingly used in gardens to destroy weeds, or so I have been told.

Chapter 3

Splicing

There are a number of splices, we shall deal with three; the Back Splice, the Eye Splice and the Lug Splice. Once you have mastered these three splices you will have an adequate working repertoire and a foundation that will allow you to attempt others.

Pre-stretched Dacron is hard and therefore not the most sympathetic of ropes with which to start learning to splice. It will pay you to seek out Dacron line that has not been pre-stretched. Ten millimetre diameter rope is a comfortable size to handle.

A Swedish fid will be invaluable. In use it is passed between the strands where you wish the tail to lie; the tail is laid in the groove of the fid and pulled into position when the fid is removed.

The first step in any splice is to unlay sufficient line to allow you to make the splice. Larger ropes will need to be unlaid a little more than smaller diameter lines. A rough guide would be an eight millimetre line unlaid for twelve times its diameter will give you five tucks, but a fourteen millimetre line will need about sixteen times its diameter to give that same number of tucks.

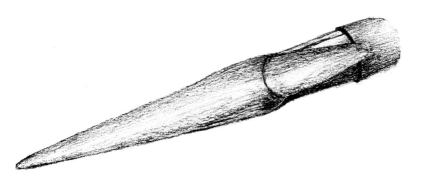

Fig 28 Swedish fid

It has been customary to use three tucks when splicing vegetable fibre ropes but man-made fibre ropes are slippery and if a man's life is to hang on the splice holding, I would suggest six tucks would be a much safer job.

Before starting to unlay a line make sure that the ends of the three strands are well sealed to prevent them unravelling. In the early stages you may find it helpful to put a seizing around the line at the point at which you aim to unlay it.

The Back Splice
We start with the back splice, which although not a particularly useful splice, is probably the simplest for the beginner to handle.

Unlay a suitable length of line and form a crown knot with the tails and pull up snug. Arrange the tails as shown in Figure 29 and it will be obvious that the tail lying along the face of the line must pass over the first strand that has not been unlaid and under the next.

Rotate the line and deal with the second and third tails in the same way.

67

Fig 29 The start of the Back Splice

The completed Back Splice

Return to the first tail, allow it to pass over the next strand and then tuck it under the following one. Do this to all three tails and continue until you have made the desired number of tucks.

Cut the ends of the tails short and seal them with a heated soldering iron or a screwdriver blade that has been heated in a gas flame.

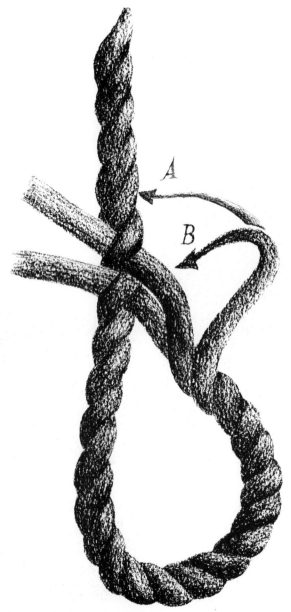

Fig 30 The start of the Eye Splice

The Eye Splice

With a suitable length of line unlaid, form a bight of the size you want and tuck the first two tails as indicated. At this stage there will be a temptation to carry on and tuck the third tail under the next strand as at 'A' in Figure 30. Do this and your splice will look like the one in the top photo below.

This third tail, 'B', must be tucked under the same strand as the first tail with the second tail between them.

*The wrong start
to an eye splice*

*The correct start
to an eye splice*

The completed Eye Splice

When all three tails have been tucked once, return to the first tail and tuck each tail in sequence until you have made as many tucks as you need.

The Lug Splice

This is a little known splice which, when mastered, can be quite useful. It will place a bight in the centre of a length of line and look quite decorative into the bargain. Its construction starts with the formation of a 'crow's foot'.

Fig 31 *Crow's Foot*

Grasp a length of line at about its centre with the thumb and forefinger of both hands just a few inches apart. Rotate the right hand in the same direction as the lay of the rope. Rotate the left hand in the opposite direction and at the same time push both hands towards each other. The result should be the crow's foot which will develop and grow as you continue to rotate the lines between your hands.

Once the parts of the crow's foot are judged to be long enough, the bight is formed and the steps that made the eye splice are followed to completion.

The start of the Lug Splice

The completed Lug Splice

There is a long splice which when properly made will join two pieces of rope so that the diameter of the rope is not increased. With vegetable fibre ropes it is commonly used, but modern rope strands do not retain their shape when unlaid and the long splice has become something very difficult, if not impossible to achieve.

Ropes that have a woven casing as their outer layer can be spliced, but I personally find the procedure lengthy and very difficult.

For ocean cruising I made up single jib sheets. After all, there is no point in exposing a redundant jib sheet to the constant chafe and damaging tropical sunshine of a two or three week ocean passage, most of which is likely to be on one tack anyway. Braidline is excellent material for jib sheets and this is what I used. In place of an eye splice, I used a racking seizing made from three millimetre line. The sheet was laid around the plastic thimble and held in place with two temporary seizings of stout thread. An end of the three millimetre line was melted onto the sheet very close to the point of the V of the thimble and a clove hitch made as additional security. This line is then passed around both parts of the sheets in a succession of figures of eight and pulled very tight until about four inches of seizing existed, when it was made off. A sacrificial covering of French whipping was added to protect the racking seizing from chafe. These 'make-believe' eye splices lasted for the life of the rope.

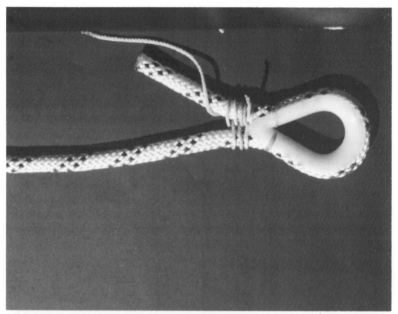

The start of my 'make-believe' eye splice.

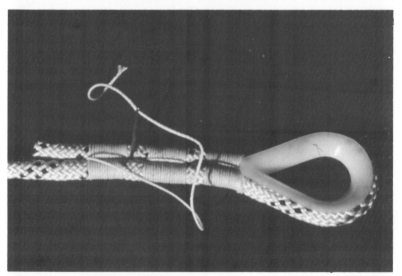

The eye lasted as long as the sheet!

Chapter 4
Mooring Lines

The basic lines required to hold a vessel against a dock wall or a pontoon are two breast ropes and two springs. The breast ropes, one fore and one aft, run from close to the bow and stern of the boat to mooring points ashore at about 90° to the fore and aft line of the vessel. Their purpose is to hold the vessel against the pontoon or wall.

The springs may be secured amidships or to fittings near the bow and stern and approach the mooring point ashore at a flat angle. Their purpose is to prevent fore and aft movement in relation to the dock. In certain circumstances two more lines may be needed, they are called bow and stern lines.

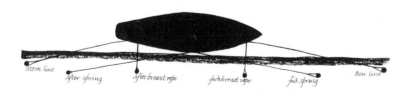

Fig 32 *Basic Mooring Lines*

The simplest mooring situation is a single vessel moored to a pontoon in windless conditions. If the stay is to be short, for example to fill the diesel tank from a pump, two breast ropes could be sufficient. For a longer stay it is sensible to rig a pair of springs to prevent the possibility of the yacht ranging back and forth in response to a passing vessel's wash.

If you are to moor alongside a vessel that is secured to a pontoon, your first step must be to fasten breast ropes to fittings on the adjacent yacht. When this is done you should rig a pair of springs, also to the yacht. By this time the two vessels are hopefully united as one and will refrain from ranging back and forth against each other in response to water movement.

Finally bow and stern lines must be secured to strong points on the pontoon. It really is gross bad manners to fail to put out fore and aft lines in this situation. Without them, the full weight of your boat and your neighbours' is taken by his cleats. Bad enough when there is only one yacht moored alongside, when six more yachts raft-up with you and also fail to rig bow and stern lines to the shore , the inside vessels are quite likely to suffer damage, especially if it comes on to blow. Not only can the inside vessels lose their cleats, but if the wind is from anywhere forward or abaft the beam the whole raft can be driven downwind and then spring back as the wind eases off. Swinging back and forth in this manner causes lines to slacken and the movement to get worse, creating considerable discomfort and the near certainty of damage.

When moored to a pontoon the tide is of little importance in as much as the pontoon rides up and down with the tide, making it unnecessary for you to tend your lines. It is a very different story when a boat is moored to an unyielding dock wall.

In my early days, a visit to Ramsgate harbour was always a minor adventure. Visiting yachts were required to lie against the outer wall of the harbour. By some special arrangement with that Irish sage named Murphy, it was always low water when we entered the harbour, which meant a thirty foot climb up a huge wooden ladders that had been built against the wall. The ladders were constructed to withstand the attention of tugs and fishing vessels and were therefore made of timbers whose dimensions were so great as to make it quite impossible for the normal human hand to gain a grip. As if to offset this disadvantage, the rungs were covered with a non slip surface of razor sharp barnacles covered by the stickiest layer of crude oil I have ever met. As the junior aboard *Avocet,* I was invariably 'specially chosen for the signal honour' of taking the lines ashore.

The harbour was always snug in a hard blow until the tide lifted the assembled craft high enough for their top hamper to rise above the harbour wall, then all hell was let loose until the tide fell away again to let the spars and rigging drop below the shelter of the wall.

When moored against a wall in tidal waters, the bow and stern lines and the springs must be long enough to allow the boat to rise and fall with the tide without adjustment and it pays to watch them until you have been through the cycle of high and low waters to make sure that you have got it right.

The breast ropes are more critical and must be tended from time to time, especially on a falling tide. To suddenly realize that you are no longer floating on water but hanging from your breast ropes is not a reassuring sensation, particularly if the tide will require another eight or ten hours before it is back to quell the flutter in your breast. Come to think of it, if you have chosen well and hung up on the highest equinoctial tide, it could take six months to return! It is interesting to note that modern designers have overcome this problem. Many boats built these days are so lightly built that the cleats would pull off the deck long before this embarrassing state of affairs arose.

When handling mooring lines remember that friction is your best friend. So often one sees a line handler trying to restrain five or ten tons of boat by hanging on to the line like grim death; you have no hope of winning that sort of battle. Take a turn or two round a nearby cleat or bollard and let the friction do the work for you, it is so much more dignified.

To 'single up' means to remove all lines except those needed to hold the vessel temporarily to the jetty, usually one or both breast ropes. The lines that remain after you have singled up should be rigged as 'slip lines' and then when you are ready to leave you can do so without assistance.

To rig a slip line the rope must be first be secured inboard and then taken around the mooring point and back again, where it is made fast. By releasing one end of the slip line you are free to move off.

Our boat is a double ender with rather flat sides amidships. Being a very heavy craft with clean lines, she carries her way for a considerable distance. In our early days with her, we would find that when coming alongside, the kindly soul who came to take our bow line would feel the urge to help *Didicoy* stop and would take a turn or two around a bollard. Snubbing her like this would cause *Didicoy* to turn 90° towards the dock, wrecking what was shaping up to be a handsome approach, one fit to draw a round of applause from the assembled dock committee. Instead we would be forced to hang our heads in shame as she came to rest with her bowsprit through the dockmaster's office window. Feeling that things could not go on like this I gave the matter some thought.

Midships on either side, *Didicoy* has a substantial cleat whose bolts go through a five inch timber. Now, when coming alongside, we ignore all offers of help and when we judge that we have slowed sufficiently a line with a large eyesplice worked into it is dropped over the chosen shoreside bollard and the other end that is led under the guard rail is turned up short on the cleat, with the result that *Didicoy* comes to a full stop flat against the pontoon.

At an exposed mooring, lines can be chafed through in short order if the weather is causing the vessel to range around. This need not be violent movement, a gentle rub throughout the night can be enough to damage or destroy a rope. A two foot length of plastic tubing slipped over and secured to the line at the danger point can give total protection.

Even the simple task of mooring a dinghy can be done well or badly, with consideration or with total disregard for others.

The line that is permanently attached to the stem of a dinghy is called a painter and it should be long enough to cope with all states of the tide. If you arrive at anything less than high water be sure to make the painter fast to an object that will still be above water when you come back!

Using a short painter at a congested landing point is positively anti-social. Get four or five dinghies tied up short and that's it, those who follow will be unable to reach the dock without clambering over the fleet of unstable dinghies. If everyone used a long painter it would be possible for us all to reach the dock without problems. Just occasionally, but not often enough, one of the short painter brigade gets his just desserts and returns to find his dinghy hanging by its nose, six feet above the water and the erstwhile contents floating out to sea.

In these days of crowded marinas it is becoming more commonplace to find yourself rafted up with other vessels, sometimes as many as a dozen abreast. The first thing to be said is that good manners requires that you pass across the foredeck of the vessels you need to cross to get ashore, thereby keeping your intrusion to a minimum.

In the days almost beyond recall, small sailing vessels that operated on the bucket and chuck-it sanitation system often used to site the bucket beneath the open forehatch to gain some headroom. If a gentleman, crossing the foredeck of such a yacht, was confronted with the top hamper of a female figure protruding from the hatch and the lady in question had a thoughtful look on her face, the form was to say 'Good morning SIR'.

The raft of yachts may be moored to a pontoon or dock or they may be moored fore and aft between posts. The steps required to extract your vessel from this situation are much the same whether you are alongside or in midstream.

Let us assume that you are lying head to tide between posts in the middle of a raft of boats. Single up to breast ropes and forward line on your own boat and warn other crews of your intentions, hopefully enlisting a measure of help from some of them.

The breast ropes of the vessels outside yours must be cast off from your cleats. The down tide ropes of those vessels blocking your escape must be removed from the post, taken around the bow of your yacht and if they are long enough, replaced on the post. You are now ready to move and this is when you will be glad that your forward line is rigged as a slip line.

With all your lines released, ease your way back and out. I hope that your manners are such that you will moor to the outside vessel and help restore order to the lines of those vessels that you are leaving behind.

Many years ago I helped a neighbouring boat get out of a raft of sixteen boats; our two vessels were the centre pair, naturally. The crew of the departing boat and I were the only occupants of this massive raft. All went without a hitch and the crew of the departing boat shouted their thanks as they went on their way, leaving me to resecure the seven boats whose stern lines I held in teeth and hands.

Chapter 5
Rope and Sail Controls

The Dutchman

There are numerous stainless-steel fittings on sale that are
intended to unite the jib sheets with the clew of the jib. This
they usually do well enough but they have a number of
drawbacks. Many of them rely on a very small spring to keep
the jaws closed and this is often made of metal that rusts or
breaks. When the jib is thrashing about, a thump with one of
these stainless steel fittings can keep your dentist in beer
money for weeks to come. And without exception they are
expensive.

We use a 'Dutchman', so called because I first saw them in
use in Holland many years ago. It consists simply of a short
length of rope with an eye splice in one end and a manrope
knot in the other. I tried it, liked it and have used one ever
since. So far it has never let me down.

In use, the eye splice is passed through the eye of the sheets
and the clew of the jib. The eye splice should be just big
enough for the manrope knot to be pushed through it.

A figure of eight knot would serve in place of the manrope
knot but perhaps not look quite so handsome.

It is not unusual to use a bowline for this purpose but a few days of hard sailing often tightens the knot to a point where it can be very difficult to release.

Boom Gallows

These seem to have gone out of fashion because the racing fraternity have jettisoned them in their everlasting quest to reduce weight and windage and the rest of the sailing world has, as in many other ways, followed blindly in their wake.

A boom gallows is an essential piece of equipment for any boat that is to go to sea. In essence it is a strong chock shaped structure to house the boom when the topping lift is eased and to hold it steady against the motion of the boat. It does not have to be a cumbersome item although it is surprising how useful they are for many other purposes. A piece of stainless steel tubing that is also part of the spray hood is one possibility. If your boat has a doghouse, a shaped block of wood that is fixed to the top of the doghouse could be the answer.

Whatever form it takes, a strong boom gallows is vital to safety to the hand who is working on the mainsail. Once the boom is settled into the gallows and the mainsheet is hauled taut and secured, the boom is transformed from a lethal weapon to a solid handrail.

Topping Lift

If you run the topping lift down the backstay instead of down the mast, it becomes possible to position the boom in the gallows without leaving the safety of the cockpit. If this method is adopted you should also be able to control the main halyard from the cockpit by running it from the mast exit via a turning block at deck level near the mast collar (if keel stepped) and thence back via a winch on the coachroof to a cleat. All mainsail controls can then be operated without climbing out of the cockpit onto the side-decks and the ensuing dance with death to reach controls affixed to the mast.

An involuntary gybe often lifts the boom end quite high, thus producing a great bight of slack line in the topping lift that can trap the boom with somewhat uncomfortable consequences. To avoid this you should seize a stainless steel ring to the backstay, three or four feet above normal boom level and run the downward pulling part of the topping lift through it.

I read somewhere that the topping lift should be of nylon rope. We followed this suggestion and cursed the author all the way across the Atlantic. Every time that we tried to raise the boom the cockpit became full with the fall of the lift and the boom refused to rise.

Lazy Jacks

In much the same way that boom gallows are seldom seen, so was the case with lazy jacks. Recently however, some sailmakers have been advertising them as though they were a unique invention, but in reality lazy jacks are a well tried system stemming from the past and which are a great boon to short-handed sailors.

In use, when the main halyard is released and the sail drops to the boom it is restrained from falling in an uncontrolable, flapping mass by the lazy jacks. They help restrain a partially lowered sail when a reef is being taken in – a time when any help is most welcome. What is more the mainsail can be dropped and forgotten when you are otherwise occupied with mooring or anchoring. The sail is so secure that we have often left it over night with no additional lashing.

Five millimetre line for lazy jacks is adequate for most boats. There are several designs. In the simplest and cheapest two lines are spliced to the topping lift and run vertically down to and round the boom and then back up to the topping lift into which they are spliced again.

There is another more recent adaptation on the theme called a 'Dutchman' – good ideas these lowlanders have, that is possibly better than the lazy jacks previously described. It requires one or more vertical lines of small reinforcing patches to be sewn into the mainsail, each with an eyelet set in it. The top ends of the lines are spliced to the topping lift and the lower end is fixed to the boom. In use, as the mainsail is lowered, so the lines cause it to flake down neatly on the boom, alternately to port and starboard.

Reefing

Initially our mainsail was furnished with a lanyard instead of reefing pendants and it was always difficult to manage in strong winds, which is of course when you want to use the system. I could never get each part of the sail secured in a uniform manner and the end of a long lanyard was forever being snatched from my hand by the wind as I worked.

At the earliest opportunity we changed to reefing points with the reef ties attached. The change was not difficult. I passed suitable lengths of line through each eyelet that had been provided for the lanyard, so that an equal length was on either side of the sail and then secured it with an overhand knot as close to the eyelet as was possible on both sides of the sail. Should you decide to do this, be generous with the length of line that you use for your reefing points. It makes reefing much easier if the points are long rather than short.

I use three strand line for one set of reefing points and bright red braided line for the other set. This has proved to be of great help in distinguishing between the two rows of points when I am struggling to get a reef tucked in. Even in the dark it is possible to determine the difference simply by the feel of the reefing points.

Each row of reefing points ends with a cringle at the leech of the sail. A reefing pendant is spliced into each of these cringles from where it descends to the boom and is then turned around a bee block. From there it is led along the boom, usually through two or three bulls eye fairleads, to the forward end where it is cleated. The end of the pendant should go through a hole in the cleat and be retained with a stopper knot.

Some boats are furnished with a small winch on the forward underside of the boom to help you pull the leech reefing eye right down. This is fine so long as it is used with understanding. Even a small winch can exert a powerful pull and if you have failed to lower the mainsail enough, the tensions created could tear the sail. If you work without a winch you are incapable of exerting sufficient power to do this and you are therefore prompted to ease the halyard.

The purpose of the pendant is to bring the leech reef cringle down to the boom and hold it there. For this purpose the line needs to be strong but if it is too heavy it will forever be pulling the leech of the sail down and spoiling its shape when sailing under full main. It is possible to use a fairly light line for the reefing pendant which helps avoid the distortion of the leech but is then far too thin to man-handle when pulling it in from the mast. I overcame this by using two diameters of line, a thin one for the vertical part and a heavier line for the horizontal part, joining them at the boom with a splice that has substantial seizing to reinforce it.

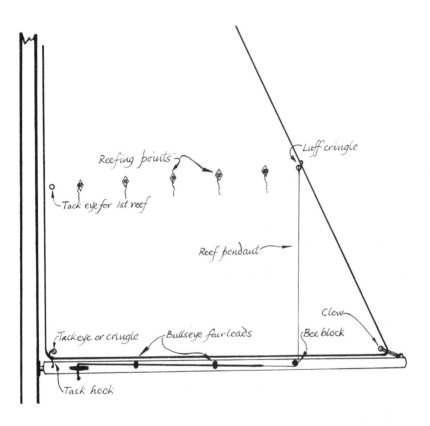

Reefing points

Luff cringle

Tack eye for 1st reef

Reef pendant

Clew

Bee block

Tack eye or cringle

Bullseye fairleads

Tack hook

Fig 33 *Mainsail Reefing System on* Didicoy

Reefing Procedure

Our first step in reefing is to head as close to the wind as possible, get the boom into the gallows and the mainsheet made up so that I can rely on the boom to keep me inboard.

The main is then lowered rather further than is needed to get the line of reefing points on to the boom. If you do not create enough slack at this stage you will create difficulties for yourself in the subsequent steps.

We, like most boats, have two large hooks welded to the goose neck which are used to attach the luff reefing cringles to the boom. There is one on each side. Once the hook is in the cringle the correct reefing pendant is used to haul the leech reefing cringle to the boom and hold it there.

So far the work has been done in the region of the mast, which with the shrouds gives a degree of security. The next step requires a move on to the coach roof to tie the pairs of reefing points under the foot of the sail. I keep a four feet long (1.3m) piece of line attached to my safety-harness which serves to fasten me to the boom and makes it possible to use both hands for reefing.

When I reach the leech cringle, I tie it to the boom with several turns of light line to back up the reefing pendant. Should the pendant be used alone, it could part or free itself under the load imposed on it and if that happened, the main would almost certainly be ripped across the line of reefing points. This light line lives on the boom, one piece for each reefing cringle so that is always at hand when needed. Finally the mainsail is rehoisted to its new setting.

When shaking a reef out, the reefing points must be the first lines to be released otherwise the sail is again exposed to the very real possibility of being ripped across its width.

The tails of all halyards must be secured at deck level. It is an immense help to be able to uncleat a halyard and forget it, knowing that the fall will not be flying at the masthead when you have subdued the sail you are lowering.

Safety-Harness

I have never been completely happy with the pattern of most of the safety-harnesses that appear in the general market place. Many are clumsy and difficult to put on in a hurry and some are still sold with a simple carbine hook that was proved highly suspect over several years. At the time when I wished to purchase a new model, only one had the approval of the British Standards Institute - I therefore decided to design and make my own.

After one or two false starts I arrived at the design that is illustrated in the accompanying photograph. I know it works well because I was wearing one on the only occasion so far, on which I have involuntarily parted company with my boat. The hook that is so unsafe for use on a lifeharness is illustrated in Figure 34 and I would advise you to steer well clear of any harnesses that include them. It has no lock to stop the jaw accidentally opening and in certain conditions, that are far from rare, it can open and fall away from the point to which it has been attached.

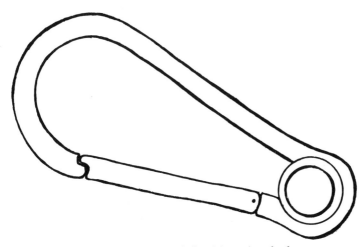

Fig 34 *The type of carbine hook that is <u>not safe</u> for use on a safety-harness.*

To make the model that is of my own design, firstly work a large eye splice into one end of a line of about 3.5 metres length and 12 to 15 millimetres diameter. The line should be a rope with a softish feel for comfort and flexibility. Experiment with a bowline to find the right size bight for your body shape and decide how much tail you want between the splice and the hook. Captive on the rope of this eyesplice must be a strong hook which can be forbidden to open accidently and yet be easily used. The splice must be big enough to allow you to place an arm and a shoulder into it and to bring the top of the eye splice across the back, under the arm and over the chest to meet the other part of the eye splice so that they can be clipped together. A small eye splice must obviously be worked into the other end of the line.

The safety-harness of my own design

Replacing a Halyard

Melt one end of both the old and new halyards and push
them together, end to end. Reinforce this with a band of
stitching and you will be ready to hoist your new halyard as
you pull the old one down.

Bulldog Grips

A few bulldog grips of a size suited to your standing rigging
wires should be carried to enable you to make a jury repair
should a shroud or stay break. The broken end of the rigging
wire can be turned back on itself and secured with two
bulldog grips to form an eye. Make a length of light line fast
to the eye and run it to the bottle screw and back to the eye
repeatedly, hauling tight every time the line passes through
the eye or the bottle screw. Finish with three or four half
hitches around the lanyard you have formed and use the
bottle screw to tighten to your satisfaction.

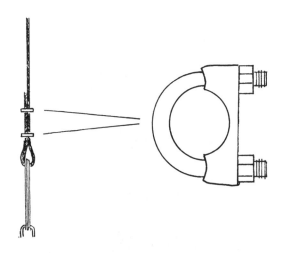

Fig 35 *Bulldog Grips*

Sheeting a Headsail from the Main Boom

When the wind is broad on the beam and both headsail and mainsail are both set to leeward, there comes a time when the jib will benefit from being poled out, but the whisker pole cannot be rigged to support the jib because the shrouds are in the way. If you have had the foresight to shackle a single sheave block to the outer end of the main boom you can rig a jib sheet as shown in the illustration.

Aboard *Didicoy* we have a length of line that runs from the goose neck, through the block at the end of the boom and then back to the goose neck – it stays there throughout the season. When the need arises it is a simple matter to release one end, pass it outside the shrouds and secure it to the clew of the jib in place of the normal jib sheet. When that is done, the other end of the line is taken to a turning block at deck level and then to the jib sheet winch where it is handled in the normal manner. When the main and jib sheets are adjusted correctly the wind fairly whistles through the slot made by the two sails.

There is no reason why a system of this kind should be confined to those occasions when the purpose made whisker pole can't be used. If you are running before the wind with the jib and main on the same side, the boom end sheet can serve perfectly well. This dodge can also be useful if you need to supplement the main and jib with a second foresail, particularly useful when the wind is on the quarter. The whisker pole will be used to pole out the jib to the windward side, braced well forward. The boom end sheet can then take care of the foresail that is set to leeward.

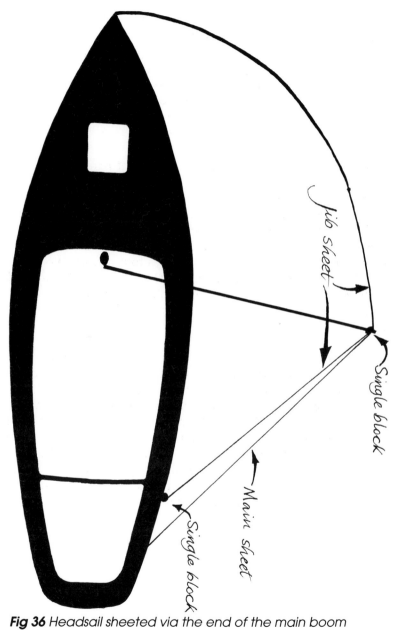

Jib sheet

Single block

Main sheet

Single block

Fig 36 *Headsail sheeted via the end of the main boom*

95

Whisker Poles

Whisker poles can either be complicated contraptions that are inordinately expensive and quite often a danger to life and limb – or fairly straightforward spars that are sensibly priced and can be used safely with a minimum of fuss. When we bought *Didicoy*, a 12 ton Hillyard, she had on board a solid wooden whisker pole with a diameter of 2½in (64mm) which had probably been put on board when she was launched some thirty years ago. We have no idea how many miles this spar served for the previous owners but we have sailed some 40,000 miles with it, much of it before the wind and it looks good for another 40,000.

Whether you invest in an expensive, state of the art pole or you follow our example and keep it simple, not to mention cheap, you must be able to rig it in safety. I have only met one system that can be worked in safety and with ease by one person; the rest need a muscle bound team of athletes.

This magic system requires a purpose made track about the length of the spar, that is fastened to the front of the mast. The slide that runs in the track has a universal joint as part of the fitting that is fixed to the inboard end of the spar.

Also on the forward face of the mast, but above the top end of the track is a single block. A halyard passes through the block and one end of the halyard is shackled to the top of the slide. The other end is shackled to the lower end of the slide and acts as a downhaul. At a convenient level the halyard passes through a jamming cleat that is screwed to the mast. This arrangement allows the slide to be raised or lowered to the full extent of the track.

Finally there must be a standing topping lift, without it the system will not work. This topping lift must go to a point a little above the top of the track and it should be comfortably taut when the pole is stowed. In order to be able to adjust the system for different sized sails, it helps to take the topping lift through a single block at the mast rather than making it of fixed length. If this line is taken through a block and down to a jamming cleat its length can be varied to accommodate sails of different sizes and clew heights. This should not however, cloud the fact that the topping lift is fixed when in use.

The investment necessary in rigging this system is money well spent. When the pole is stowed it sits against the front of the mast with its inboard end near the top of the track. An eye should be fixed to the mast, just below the track, to accept the jaws at the outward (lower) end of the pole to hold it secure against movement.

In use the jaw on the outboard end of the pole is released from its retaining eye and the downhaul pulled until the outboard end of the pole reaches the guard rail. At this point the pole is lifted over the rail and is allowed to rest in the angle between the guard rail and the foremost shroud. The next step is to open the piston and place the jib sheet into the jaw.

With plenty of slack in the jib sheet the pole can be raised to the horizontal and the sheet hauled in to its approximate sheeting position. You will notice that the jib has not been involved so far and this means that there has been no wind pressure on the gear whilst it has been handled, with the consequent result that there is absolutely no hassle. Indeed the task throughout is so lacking in drama, that even in the worst weather the need for muscle does not arise. It remains to hoist the jib and adjust sheets as necessary.

There are two points worth reiterating. The first is that the standing topping lift is at the heart of the system and it cannot work without one. (See Figs 37 A, B, C.) The second is that once the jib sheet is in the jaw of the pole, it can be pulled in but not hauled tight, or it will be impossible to adjust the pole and it may also make it difficult to hoist the headsail.

A third point is to emphasis that the sheet and not the clew of the sail is placed in the pole jaws. This makes the operation much easier and will also allow the pole to accommodate sails of different sizes. The sheet will not suffer when used like this, as the parts of the jaw are so smooth and rounded that there is no possibility of chafe. We have sailed many thousands of miles rigged like this with no wear on the sheets at this point.

When the pole is no longer required, a simple pull on the line that opens the jaws will allow the sheet to fall out. The pole is then free to be stowed and the jib to be adjusted to the new situation.

We have found that a fore guy and a preventer are well worth rigging. The fore guy runs from the outboard end of the pole forward and the preventer runs from the pole end aft. With these two additional lines rigged the whole thing is secure even if the boat gybes involuntarily.

Fig 37 ➡

In A, the inner end of the whisker pole lies almost at the top of the mast track and the bottom (outer) end has been released from its retaining clip. As the mast slide downhaul is applied, the fixed topping lift forces the outer end of the pole outwards and upwards. At stage B, with the pole resting on the guard-rail, the jib sheet is placed in the jaws.

Further application of the downhaul will automatically push the pole outwards and bring it to its working height at C.

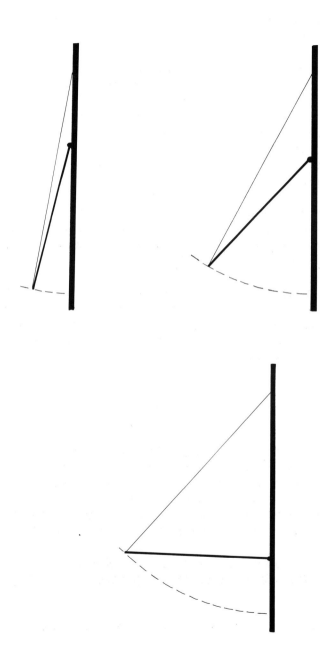

Chapter 6
Towing and Manoeuvring with Lines

Towing
In calm water it pays to tow another vessel, or perhaps your own with your dinghy, from alongside. This gives much greater control than towing from ahead. If there is a lop in the water towing from ahead is likely to be the answer, as the movement between the two vessels could cause damage to one or other. Towing alongside and towing from ahead are two different techniques and we shall deal with them separately.

Towing from Ahead
Even in sheltered waters avoid the temptation to use a short tow-line. The towed vessel needs to be able to stay well clear of the tug's stern if accidents are to be avoided. In anything but the calmest of situations it will pay to protect the tow-line from chafe. Plastic tubing slipped onto the line and secured in place will give a large measure of protection.

Ideally the tow-line should be secured to the towed vessel at about the mast, (the same applies to the tug – if only the fore and back stays were not in the way!) as it would give much greater manoeuvrability than towing from stern to stem. A boat pivots at a point generally just abaft the mast and to tie it down at bow or stern does nothing to help directional control.

However, a co-operative movement between the two vessels can help considerably. If the tug slows slightly, so that the load comes off the tow-line, it will be easier for her to turn and the towed vessel can then follow in its wake. If this is not effective or the turn is to be a tight one, the towed vessel can help initially by turning the wrong way, thereby forcing the towing boat's stern round in the desired direction. If the stern goes to starboard the bow must go to port. As can be seen, this means that both helmsmen must know the score and it would probably help for a crew member to relay instructions to the towed vessel by VHF.

If the tow is taking place in the open sea, the tow-line must be long enough to create sufficient catenary to the line to allow one or both vessels to lift or fall to the seas without constantly snubbing the line. The elasticity inherent in nylon line can also help to reduce snubbing. The best plan for a long tow in anything but the calmest conditions, is for the towed yacht's anchor to be unshackled and the anchor chain to be used for at least part of the tow-line. This has two advantages. The cable will not be prone to chafe and its weight will help greatly in preventing the damage of snubbing that is bound to occur if there is a sea running. The chain is likely to graze the towed boat's toerail if steps are not taken to prevent it.

Towing from Alongside

This is by far the preferred method if circumstances permit as it allows much more directional and speed control.

The dinghy or inflatable, if that is what is to be used as the tug, must be lashed alongside the boat to be towed so that both the sterns are level, this will give good steering control. Breast ropes and springs should be rigged with minimum slack. By using two springs a measure of stopping power is gained, assuming that the tug can generate reverse thrust.

In our early sailing days most of us are guilty of trying to solve many of the problems that arise at sea by the use of sheer brute strength. As one gains that special experience which only comes with sea miles under the belt, it gradually dawns on all but the most daft of mariners, that one can call upon more elegant and seamanlike methods of going about things. In the days of commercial and naval sail, where the loads were so great that they could not be controlled by man's muscle alone, the purer form of seamanship , that of considered anticipation was formed. Along with that came the skilful use of blocks and tackles, the invention of the winch and above all an instinctive appreciation of wind and water. Using natural laws of energy and physics was and still is a fundamental part of the craftsmanship of the true seaman.

Springing a boat on or off a jetty, using wind and tide to its best advantage when mooring are all aspects of a long tradition. Likewise the anticipation of a helmsman when arriving at or departing from a mooring follows in the footsteps of good seamanship, rather than the brash fellow who simply steers his way in without thought for wind, tide or his own vessel's capabilities.

Departing a Berth Using Tide

What could be simpler when lying head to tide and hemmed in by other boats ahead and astern than to ease your way out as shown in Figures 38 A,B and C? Single up to a bow line that is rigged as a slip rope. When you are ready to move put the rudder hard over away from the jetty. As soon as the boat has moved far enough from the dock, cast of the slip line and move ahead under engine or sail.

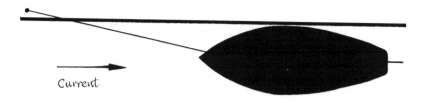

Current

Fig 38A

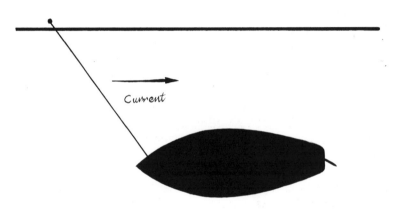

Current

Fig 38B

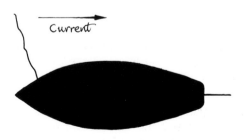

Current

Fig 38C

Springing On and Off a Jetty

Sometimes in tight circumstances it is possible to get a bow
line ashore but the stern line will not reach the dock. In
this situation, as soon as the forward line is secured put
the rudder hard over away from the shore, drive the boat
ahead with the engine against the bow line and the stern
will swing in.

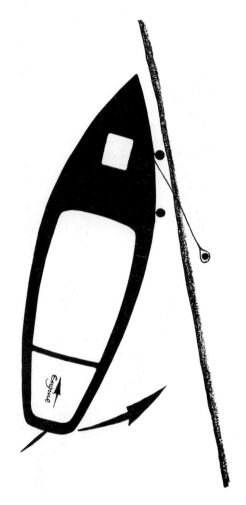

Fig 39A

If it is the bow line that has not reached the shore, use the same drill to bring it alongside by driving forward against the stern line with the rudder hard over towards the dock.

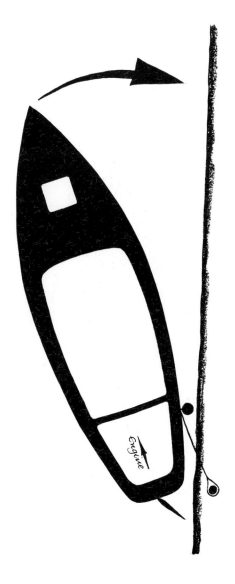

Fig 39B

When leaving a berth, the same principle can be used to move your bow or stern away from the jetty to clear any obstruction ahead or astern. The important thing to remember is that a boat does not turn in the way that a car turns, but it pivots around a point somewhere near the centre of the immersed profile of the hull.

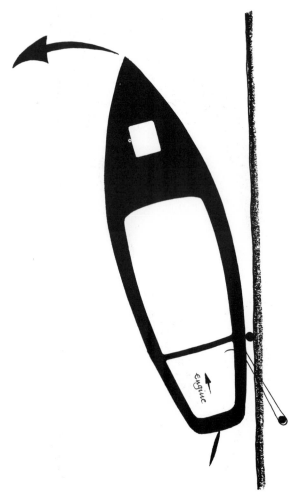

Fig 39C

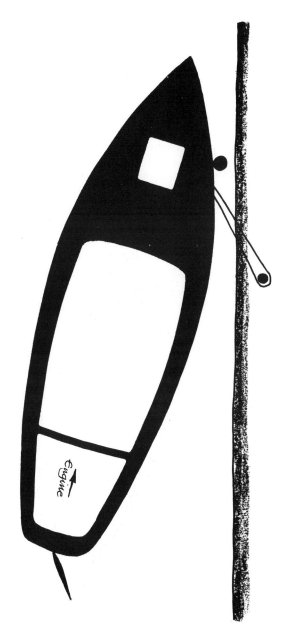

Fig 39D

Propeller Effect

Under engine most boats will turn better in one direction than in the other. This is due to a phenomenon known as 'propeller effect' (sometimes 'paddle wheel effect') which is caused by the lower blade of the propeller being more effective than the top blade. This unequal behaviour between the upper and lower blades arises because the water nearer the surface can disperse away from the blade faster than the water around the lower blade. This results in more thrust being developed in the bottom cycle of the rotation of the blade and the corresponding directional performance will depend upon whether the blade rotates to the left or right.

If your engine manual does not advise you, experiment to find out if your boat tends to steer left or right and keep the result in mind when manoeuvering so that it can help rather than hinder.(When going astern, reverse the direction of the effect)

Our own boat turns much better to starboard than to port and the effect is most marked when *Didicoy* is moving through the water at her slowest. In these circumstances full rudder and a strong burst of engine will kick her to starboard like a top – a most useful facility.

Tide and Current

The approach to an alongside berth must always be made with the likely effect of tidal stream or current in mind.

A three knot current travelling in the same direction as a boat that is making four knots through the water results in a speed over the ground of seven knots. If the vessel is turned and heads into the current her speed over the ground is reduced to one knot. By reducing her speed from four to three knots through the water she will be stemming the tide and therefore be stationary in relation to the ground and jetty. This is the main reason why it is always advisable to make your final approach to a mooring against the current whenever that option is open.

A current that flows at an angle to the pontoon at which you aim to berth can cause problems if the approach is not planned and carried out with understanding. It must be remembered that no matter which way your bow is pointing, the path over the sea bed taken by the boat will always be a combination of your speed and direction through the water, and the direction and speed of the water that you are floating in.

There is a marina that I know only too well, where the current is deflected by a small island and approaches the pontoon at an angle of at least fifteen degrees. At times it runs quite fast and provides an infinite source of entertainment for those who are already safely moored. The triangle of velocities shows what happens and it follows that your approach must be modified to counter the effect of the stream.

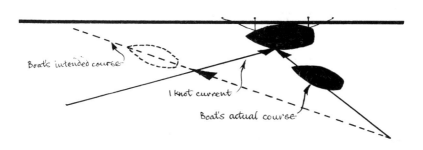

Boats intended course

1 knot current

Boat's actual course

Fig 40 *The effect of an angled current when approaching a berth*

109

When berthing head to current, if it is your lucky day, you can astound the dock committee by travelling sideways to your berth but it does require windless conditions, forethought and a measure of good luck. When you do pull it off, your satisfaction will know no bounds. Sadly, on the very few occasions I have achieved this small miracle of seamanship, the dock committee had invariably taken a break.

All that is required is to turn head to stream just off from your chosen space, match your boat speed to counter the current and turn very slightly towards the pontoon. One small reservation however, if the wind is squarely onshore it will help, but from any other direction it is likely to hinder.

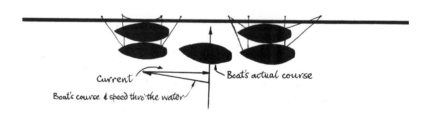

Fig 41 Uptide berthing

Winding Ship

Occasionally it is necessary to turn a boat that is lying alongside a jetty end-for-end. If two lines are rigged as shown in the illustration, and when all is ready you cast off her mooring lines, as you take in the slack in the two lines she will turn her other side to the jetty. The handling lines will in effect become new breast ropes.

Note the state of the wind and tide before you rig the lines. It will be your desire to have them work with you and not against you. If need be you can rig the lines so that the bow turns out instead of the stern.

This is a very simple manoeuvre easily carried out by one person, but please don't make your first attempt when the tide is in full spate or the wind is blowing a hooligan.

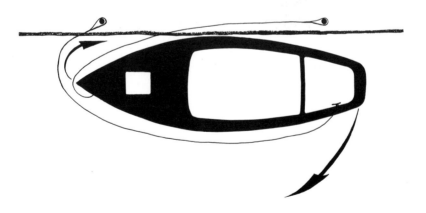

Fig 42 *Winding Ship*

Chapter 7

Ropes and Mechanical Advantage

Winches

I started sailing before winches appeared on small boats. Sails were hoisted by hauling on the halyard directly and in larger vessels blocks and tackles were used to ease the task of the man on the halyard. Halyards were always given the final hardening up by a process called 'swigging' and it is so effective that I still find myself using it. To swig a halyard, the sail is first raised just as it would be if a winch was to be used for the final touch. Once the sail is up a turn is taken on the cleat and then the halyard is pulled at right angles away from the mast. The slack gained like this is taken up on the cleat and the operation is repeated a couple of times. It is surprisingly efficient.

Sheets are something else. The mechanical advantage required to control them was always gained by using blocks and tackles; in smaller vessels it may even have been left to brute force alone. It is here that winches have wrought such a change. The comparative ease with which a sheet can now be controlled has reduced the muscle power needed and allowed the ladies to join the gentlemen.

Winches range from the simple single speed to the multiple gear, self-tailing models. They are all worked with a short lever of one kind or another. Movement on the lever causes the winch barrel to rotate and the mechanical advantage is created by the difference in the length of the lever and the radius of the winch barrel. A pawl allows the barrel to rotate in one direction only and with sufficient turns of line around the winch barrel, what is gained is retained. A further degree of advantage is gained by those models that include a system of gears.

Riding Turn

The winch is subject to one problem – the riding turn, which can be caused in a variety of ways. The result is always the same, several turns of line around the winch barrel with one or more trapped under the turn that leads to the jib. When this happens the weight of the sail, full of wind, is brought to bear on the trapped turns and there is no way that they can be freed until the load is removed from them. There are several ways to achieve this end and they will be discussed shortly, but first let us think in terms of avoiding all riding turns because they do not happen by accident; every riding turn is man-made!

The correct positioning of the winch and the correct approach (or lead) of the sheet to the winch barrel are vital. Things must be so arranged that the sheet rises to meet the winch barrel. A sheet that leads horizontally, or worse still downwards to the barrel, is a sure-fire recipe for a riding turn. It helps too, if the tail of the sheet can leave the winch barrel at a slight angle rather than a steep one. If you use a bargee hitch to secure your sheets, this latter source of trouble can be avoided.

A 'helpful' deck hand hauling on the jib sheet somewhere between the clew of the sail and the winch can also create problems. Too many turns on the winch barrel before there is tension on the sheet is another popular way to create riding turns. One or two round turns on the barrel are enough until the initial slack is gathered in by hand and until you need the power of the winch to be utilised.

Occasionally in a strong wind, a sheet that has slack in it will allow the headsail to flog badly whilst tacking. The wildly gyrating sheet can then wrap a few extra turns onto the barrel and result in a riding turn the moment the sail fills again. This last trick can also include some of the winch operator's fingers which, to say the least, will make his eyes water.

To free a riding turn, and perhaps some fingers too, the weight of the jib must be taken off the sheet at the winch. This is done by attaching a length of line to the jammed sheet somewhere between the clew of the sail and the winch. The tail of the relieving line is then taken to another winch and tightened until it has taken the load from the sheet, which will allow you to unravel the mess. A rolling hitch or a camel hitch would serve but the seamanlike answer is to pass a stopper. Unlike the two knots, a stopper will almost fall apart as soon as the load is removed from it, which could be an advantage in the fraught atmosphere that usually accompanies a riding turn.

Stopper

Using a suitable length of line make a half hitch with one end around the sheet and then wind some of the remaining line around the sheet in a loose spiral, finally lead the tail to another winch.

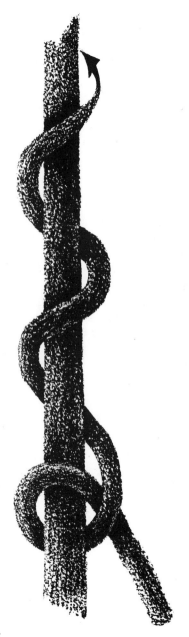

Fig 43 *A Stopper*

Spanish Windlass

If a second winch cannot be used, a form of 'Spanish Windlass' can be made. This is a device that will give you a considerable mechanical advantage with the minimum of gear. I suppose it is fair to say that it is more a principle than a specific knot and for this reason it can take a number of forms. I suspect its name originated from the old Spanish custom of garrotting those who offended them.

Figure 44 shows the form of Spanish Windlass that is most likely to be suited to the riding turn situation.

Fig 44 *The Spanish Windlass*

With a stopper clapped on the sheet take the tail of the stopper to a strong point and make it fast with a little slack in it. Somewhere about midway lay a short length of broom handle, a circular section winch handle or some similar object across the relieving line as shown. Insert a lever in the bight and rotate the lever.

The same treatment can be accorded to an anchor chain that has jammed on a winch barrel or in the naval pipe. Do remember the great forces that you are dealing with when trying to make good a foul up of this kind and keep your hands well clear of the danger area or you could find yourself sailing single-handed for the rest of your life.

Another form of Spanish Windlass that can fit other circumstances is made as follows. Secure a line to a fixed point. From there take it to the load that is to be moved towards that fixed point, secure it and return the line back to the fixed point. Insert a bar between the two lines at about the mid point and rotate the bar end-for-end. This will cause the two lines to wrap themselves around each other thus shortening the lines and giving a large mechanical advantage.(See Fig 45)

On one occasion when we were hauling *Didicoy* out, she settled at a considerable angle to the centre of the cradle. We secured a 1in (25mm) diameter line to a post on the cradle, passed the end around Didicoy's mast and back to the post where it was made fast again. A two foot length (60cm) of timber was inserted between the two lines and rotated and twelve tons of boat was slewed into its correct position by the muscle power of just one man.

Fig 45 *This system of Spanish Windlass slewed 12 Tons of boat!*

Tackles and Mechanical Advantage

Before the advent of the sheet and halyard winch, the main source of mechanical advantage in a boat was the block and tackle, sometimes called a purchase. One seldom hears 'tackle' pronounced as 'taykle' these days. The old pronunciation was probably acquired from the Dutch and it is a pity to see it disappear. The one purchase we can be sure to find in all but the smallest sailing vessel is the main sheet, with which the mainsail is controlled.

By arranging blocks and rope in a particular fashion it becomes possible to gain considerable mechanical advantage. There are dozens of specific tackles that were in regular use in the days of commercial sail, but it is sufficient for us to understand only the principles and to be able to apply them should the need arise.

In the illustrations that follow the mechanical advantage gained is stated as if friction did not exist. Unfortunately it does exist and will reduce the advantage, but the gain is still well worth having. If the sheave in the block is of too small a diameter for the rope that is being used , the tight turn around the sheave will create an unreasonable amount of friction, so the rule is – big is best.

In a tackle one block is secured to a fixed point and the other is free to move, bringing the load with it.

There is no mechanical advantage in Figure 46. The fixed block acts simply as a turning block allowing you to apply your strength in a more convenient direction, for example to lift a gas bottle or a can of diesel aboard from the tender.

Fig 46 *No mechanical advantage*

The tackle in Figure 47 gives a twofold gain. The same gear rigged as in Figure 48 gives a threefold gain and is known as using a tackle to advantage. When a tackle is used as in Figure 47 it is said to be used to disadvantage.

Obviously it is good practice to use a tackle as in Figure 48 rather than as in Figure 47, but sometimes circumstances dictate that a purchase must be used to disadvantage to allow the operator to pull in the most convenient direction.

Fig 47

Fig 48

The mechanical advantage gained by a tackle, ignoring friction, is the same as the number of parts of the rope at the moving block. Naturally there is a price to pay and to gain a twofold advantage it is necessary to pull twice as much line through the blocks as the distance travelled by the load, three times for a threefold gain and so on.

In Figure 49, two threefold tackles are used together and the gain is ninefold. To find the mechanical advantage when two tackles are rigged like this the power gained by one tackle is multiplied by the power gained by the other.

Some sheet to tiller self-steering arrangements call for a reduction in power and this is achieved by using a purchase 'back to front' which, for obvious reasons is referred to as a 'fool's tackle'.

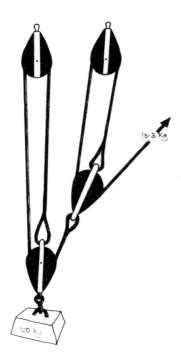

Fig 49

Waggoner's Hitch

There are two forms of a knot called a waggoner's hitch that will operate in the same way as a purchase but without the need to use blocks. (Figs 50,51) The illustrations should be self explanatory.

Fig 50 *The Waggoner's Hitch*

This useful hitch will certainly double your power at least and is a boon when lashing a dinghy down or securing a cover. The failure to use blocks to turn the rope creates extra friction of course, but the gain is still well worth having.

Fig 51 *An adaptation of the Waggoner's Hitch*

Frapping Turns

These can help to tighten the lines that are holding
something like a dinghy or life-raft in place. Imagine a dinghy
on the foredeck held in place by two athwartship lines. You
have hauled the two lashings as taut as you can get them
but you are not satisfied that they are tight enough.

Take another lighter length of line and secure it to the middle
of one of the lashings, pass it under the other lashing and
then back to the first. Repeat this four or five times, pulling
hard each time the line is passed under a lashing, as if you
were trying to get the two parts to meet.

Index